ZR AC

# DEADLY
## BATTLE OF THE WILDERNESS
# INFERNO

D1089587

## ABNETT • VANSANT • VERMA

OSPREY
GRAPHIC
HISTORY

First published in Great Britain in 2007 by Osprey Publishing,
Midland House, West Way, Botley, Oxford OX2 0PH, UK
443 Park Avenue South, New York, NY 10016, USA
E-mail: info@ospreypublishing.com

A CIP catalog record for this book is available from the British Library

ISBN 978 1 84603 052 9

Page layout by Osprey Publishing
Map by The Map Studio
Printed in China through Bookbuilders

07 08 09 10 11   10 9 8 7 6 5 4 3 2 1

FOR A CATALOG OF ALL BOOKS PUBLISHED BY OSPREY PUBLISHING
PLEASE CONTACT:

NORTH AMERICA
Osprey Direct, c/o Random House Distribution Center, 400 Hahn Road,
Westminster, MD 21157
E-mail: info@ospreydirect.com

ALL OTHER REGIONS
Osprey Direct UK, P.O. Box 140 Wellingborough, Northants, NN8 2FA, UK
E-mail: info@ospreydirect.co.uk

www.ospreypublishing.com

# CONTENTS

# WHO'S WHO

**General Robert E. Lee** (1807–70) was commander of all Southern forces as general in chief. At the Wilderness, Lee's forces were vastly outnumbered, with 123,000 Union troops, compared to 65,000 Confederates.

**Lieutenant General Ulysses S. Grant** (1822–85) was named general in command of the Union army in 1864. Despite heavy losses at the Wilderness, Grant fought Lee aggressively until the war's end.

**Brigadier General Micah Jenkins** (1839–64) was a heroic Confederate officer. He was shot in the forehead during the battle of the Wilderness, but left the field cheering on his men.

**Major General Gouverneur K. Warren** (1830–82) and his corps saw important action at the Wilderness. Warren also played a key role in the Union victory at Gettysburg in July 1863.

# THE AMERICAN CIVIL WAR 1861–65

The American Civil War officially began on April 12, 1861, when Southern forces attacked Fort Sumter, a federal fort in South Carolina. The attack came after many years of anger and disagreement between Northern and Southern states. The main disagreement was over the issue of slavery. Slavery was legal in the South and illegal in the North. The U.S. government tried to pass laws to deal with these differences, but a good solution could not be agreed to.

In 1860, Abraham Lincoln, an anti-slavery candidate, won the presidential election. The South felt threatened by Lincoln's victory. Soon after the election, South Carolina seceded, or left, the Union. More Southern states followed. These states formed the Confederate States of America, a separate government.

The four years of terrible fighting that followed the attack on Fort Sumter tested the strength of the young nation – and nearly destroyed the Union. Many horrible battles were fought, but perhaps none was more terrifying than the battle fought in Virginia in late 1864, known simply as "The Wilderness." ■

# INTO THE WILDERNESS

After three years of bloody combat, the American Civil War continued to drag on. From the opening shots of the war fired by Confederate forces on Fort Sumter in April 1861, to the historic struggles at First Bull Run, Shiloh, Antietam, Chancellorsville, Gettysburg, and many other places, Northern and Southern forces still waged bitter battle against one other.

By 1864, Confederate forces were badly suffering from lack of supplies, including food and clothing. Their number of men was shrinking, due to losses on the battlefields and a generally smaller male population than that in the North. The Union army, however, was much better

Ulysses S. Grant had become the most successful Union general by the time of the battle of the Wilderness. He became president of the United States in 1867. (Courtesy of Library of Congress) ▼

fed and supplied—and had been since the beginning of the conflict.

The Union army also had the advantage of leadership. Although General George Meade was still officially in command of the Union army, Ulysses S. Grant had become its driving force. Earlier in the war, he had defeated Confederate forces in critical battles in Tennessee. Grant strongly believed in his own ability to command—a trait that no previous commander of the Union army had shown.

In the winter of 1863–64, the Rapidan River in Virginia separated the Union and Confederate armies in the East. Confederate General Robert E. Lee's Army of Northern Virginia spent much of that winter camped on one side of the river. On the other side, Grant's Union army was preparing to cross the river and attack the Confederate forces close to their heart—the Confederate capital of Richmond, Virginia.

By the time Grant crossed the river on May 4, 1864, his forces numbered about

▲

The Wilderness ran to the edge of the Rapidan River. The thick, heavy woodland made the fight between Grant and Lee one of the toughest battles of the American Civil War. (Courtesy of Library of Congress)

120,000 men. Lee's army was about half that number. Grant's plan was to move straight through an area known as the Wilderness to get between his enemy and Richmond. He wisely never planned to do battle there.

But when Lee learned that Grant had crossed the Rapidan, he quickly attacked his enemy. The Wilderness, a 70-square-mile area of thickets, scrub growth, and rough terrain, was to become the hellish nightmare that Grant desperately wanted to avoid.

General Grant crossed the Rapidan River over this pontoon bridge that his men built. When General Lee found out about General Grant's crossing, he gave his Confederate forces the order to attack the Union immediately. (Courtesy of Library of Congress)

▼

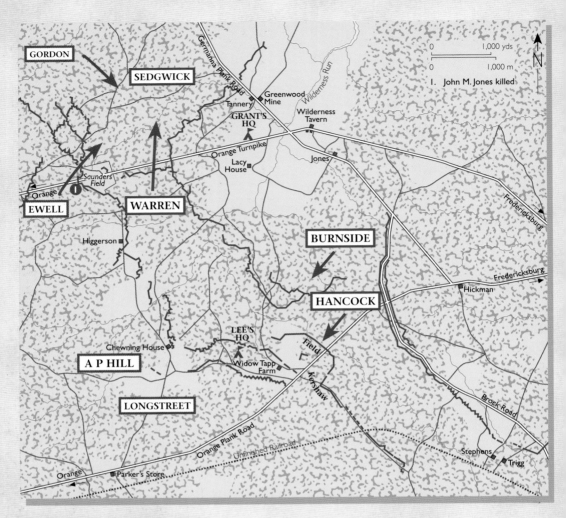

GORDON

SEDGWICK

Germanna Plank Road

Greenwood Mine

Tannery

Wilderness Run

GRANT'S HQ

Wilderness Tavern

Orange Turnpike

Lacy House

Jones

Saunders Field

Orange

EWELL

WARREN

Higgerson

BURNSIDE

Fredericksburg

Fredericksburg

Hickman

HANCOCK

Chewning House

LEE'S HQ

Field

A P HILL

Widow Tapp Farm

Kershaw

LONGSTREET

Brock Road

Orange Plank Road

Unfinished Railroad

Stephens

Trigg

Orange

Parker's Store

0        1,000 yds

0        1,000 m

1.   John M. Jones killed

N

# TWO DAYS OF FIGHTING

Once Lee attacked Grant's forces, the advantages the Union had outside the Wilderness were lost. Because there were few roads in the heavily wooded area, Grant's superior numbers of men and artillery meant very little.

Each army made one attack after another against its opponent on May 5 and 6. Artillery explosions and gunshots eventually set the woods on fire, turning the area into a blazing inferno. Many men were burned

After stalemate skirmishing between forces near Orange Turnpike on May 5, General Hancock and his men came out fighting the next day, shattering General A.P. Hill's line across the Orange Plank Road. The Confederates were in trouble until General Longstreet arrived to relieve Hill and "rolled up the Union line like a wet blanket." Burnside arrived to support Hancock and the fight went on until darkness fell. Raging fires put an end to the battle.

to death. The choking smoke created a fog so thick that soldiers could barely see what—or whom—they were shooting at.

At the end of the first day of fighting, Union forces were on the verge of overpowering the enemy. But the Confederates held out. The Confederates spent a sleepless night, knowing that they could not withstand another serious assault in the morning. Yet despite the horrors of that first day, neither army's position had changed. The Confederates held the western edge of the battlefield, and the Union held the eastern edge.

The desperate Confederates were saved by the arrival of General James Longstreet's troops on the morning of May 6. Heavy fighting marked the second day as both armies continued to pound at each other. The Confederates, however, nearly lost Longstreet—Lee's number one general —when a Confederate volley of gunfire accidentally ripped into a group of Confederate officers. Longstreet was badly wounded and out of action for months.

▲

Much of the fighting in the Wilderness was done from behind trees, as soldiers tried to shoot at the enemy, without hitting their own men. The thick woods, rough terrain, and blazing fires made the battlefield a sea of confusion. (Winslow Homer © The New Britain Museum of American Art)

In a letter to his parents, a soldier at the Wilderness said of the fighting, "We see hundreds of wounded by the sides of the road and the wounded in the ambulances are screeching as they are moved off the field." (Gerry Embleton © Osprey Publishing Ltd)

▼

By the end of the second day of fighting, Confederate forces inflicted terrible damage on the Union army. After two days of fighting, Grant had lost about 18,000 men. Lee's losses were about 8,000. The Union narrowly avoided total defeat and had not even gained an inch of ground for all their losses.

But Grant was a leader who was willing to take the fight to his enemy—and the first Union army commander willing to sacrifice large numbers of soldiers to bring the war to an end. Despite the terrible loss at the Wilderness, Grant continued his pursuit of Lee.

# THE BATTLE OF THE WILDERNESS

ON MARCH 9, 1864, ULYSSES S. GRANT WAS MADE A LIEUTENANT GENERAL AND PUT IN CHARGE OF THE UNION ARMY.

WE WILL HAMMER CONTINUOUSLY AGAINST THE ENEMY UNTIL THERE SHALL BE NOTHING LEFT FOR HIM, SIR.

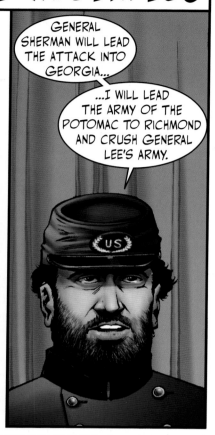

GENERAL SHERMAN WILL LEAD THE ATTACK INTO GEORGIA...

...I WILL LEAD THE ARMY OF THE POTOMAC TO RICHMOND AND CRUSH GENERAL LEE'S ARMY.

GRANT'S ARMY OF THE POTOMAC WAS STRONG, WELL FED, AND VERY ORGANIZED. HE COMMANDED OVER 100,000 MEN AND LED A SUPPLY TRAIN OF 400 WAGONS.

THE CONFEDERATE ARMY OF NORTHERN VIRGINIA HAD SPENT A HARD WINTER CAMPED IN ORANGE COUNTY, VIRGINIA. THEY WERE SHORT ON SUPPLIES. SOME CONFEDERATE SOLDIERS HAD DESERTED.

CONFEDERATE COMMANDER, GENERAL LEE, HAD AN ARMY OF ABOUT 60,000 MEN.

THE ARMY OF THE POTOMAC WILL CROSS THE RAPIDAN RIVER AND MARCH TO RICHMOND. WE MUST STOP THEM BY ATTACKING THEM HERE.

GENERAL LEE PLANNED TO ATTACK THE UNION ARMY IN AN OVERGROWN WOODED AREA CALLED THE WILDERNESS. IN THE THICK FOREST, THE ENEMY'S GREATER NUMBERS WOULD NOT BE SUCH AN ADVANTAGE.

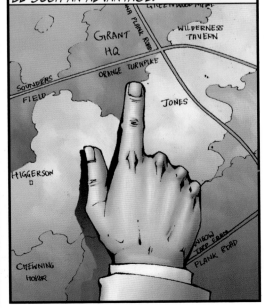

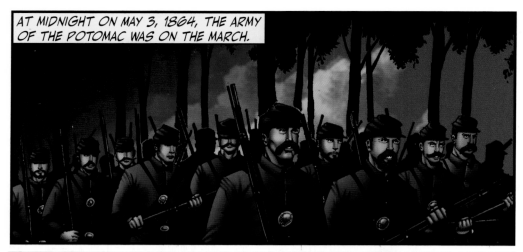

AT MIDNIGHT ON MAY 3, 1864, THE ARMY OF THE POTOMAC WAS ON THE MARCH.

ONCE WE'VE CROSSED THE RIVER, WE'VE STILL GOT TO GET THROUGH THOSE WOODS.

AS LONG AS THE REBELS DON'T KNOW WE'RE COMING, WE'LL BE ON SAFE GROUND BEFORE WE FIGHT.

BY MIDDAY ON MAY 4, MOST OF THE UNION TROOPS HAD CROSSED THE RIVER. BY NIGHTFALL, THEY WERE CAMPED ON THE SOUTH BANK OF THE RIVER AND ALONG THE GERMANNA PLANK ROAD.

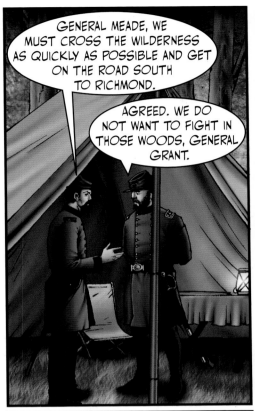

AT DAWN ON MAY 5, CONFEDERATE FORCES MADE THEIR WAY TOWARD THE BROCK ROAD AND THE ENEMY.

MAY 5, 6:00 A.M. UNION SOLDIERS FROM V CORPS WERE ON THE MARCH WHEN THEY SPOTTED THE CONFEDERATE TROOPS.

GENERAL EWELL HAS ENGAGED THE ENEMY ON THE TURNPIKE ABOUT A MILE NORTH OF HERE. WE ARE JOINED IN BATTLE, GENTLEMEN.

WHEN GENERAL MEADE RECEIVED NEWS OF THE FIGHTING HE WAS NOT ALARMED.

THIS IS NO MORE THAN A REARGUARD ACTION. THE MAIN REBEL FORCE HAS ALREADY RETREATED OUT OF OUR PATH.

FIGHTING ON THE TURNPIKE SOON TURNED TO FULL-SCALE SKIRMISHING IN THE SURROUNDING WOODLAND.

IT WAS EVERY MAN FOR HIMSELF.

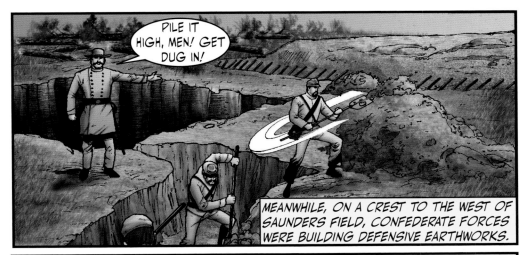

MEANWHILE, ON A CREST TO THE WEST OF SAUNDERS FIELD, CONFEDERATE FORCES WERE BUILDING DEFENSIVE EARTHWORKS.

UNION GENERAL GOUVERNEUR K. WARREN LED THE INFANTRY OF V CORPS ONTO THE EAST SIDE OF SAUNDERS FIELD.

GENERAL EWELL'S CONFEDERATE TROOPS OPENED FIRE.

CONFEDERATE GUNFIRE MOWED DOWN THE UNION FORCES AS THEY CLIMBED THE RIDGE TOWARD THE CONFEDERATES.

WHEN UNION FORCES REACHED THE CONFEDERATE EARTHWORKS THEY TRIED TO BREACH THE CONFEDERATE LINE.

CHARGE!

CONFEDERATE GENERAL JOHN M. JONES WAS KILLED IN THE UNION ATTACK.

CONFEDERATE REINFORCEMENTS ARRIVED. THEY SOON DROVE THE UNION SOLDIERS BACK.

IF ANY OPPORTUNITY PRESENTS ITSELF FOR PITCHING INTO A PART OF LEE'S ARMY, WE MUST DO SO.

WHEN GENERAL GRANT WAS NOTIFIED OF THE FIERCE FIGHTING, HE WAS READY TO ACT.

15

CONFEDERATE GENERAL AMBROSE HILL MARCHED HIS TROOPS ALONG THE ORANGE PLANK ROAD, A MILE SOUTH OF SAUNDERS FIELD, TO HEAD OFF THE ENEMY.

UNION FORCES HAD STARTED TO CROSS THE WILDERNESS ALONG THE BROCK ROAD. THE CONFEDERATES HOPED TO CRUSH THEM AT THE JUNCTIONS WITH THE ORANGE TURNPIKE AND THE ORANGE PLANK ROAD.

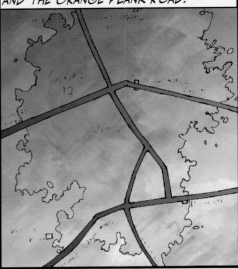

UNION CAVALRY WHO WERE FIRST OUT OF THE WOODS ENGAGED WITH GENERAL HILL'S TROOPS ON THE ORANGE PLANK ROAD. FIERCE FIGHTING BROKE OUT.

UNION GENERAL WINFIELD S. HANCOCK WAS SOON JOINED IN THE BATTLE BY UNION GENERAL GEORGE GETTYS AND HIS INFANTRY.

GENERALS HILL AND HANCOCK FOUGHT A BITTER BATTLE.

KRAK! KRAK! KRAK!

KILL THE REBELS!

SOLDIERS FELL BACK AND SKIRMISHED IN THE THICK UNDERGROWTH OF THE WILDERNESS. HUNDREDS WERE WOUNDED AND KILLED ON BOTH SIDES.

KRAK! KRAK! KRAK!

IT WAS IMPOSSIBLE TO SEE WHERE THE ENEMY'S LINES WERE. FIGHTING BROKE DOWN INTO SMALL SKIRMISHES ALL OVER THE WILDERNESS.

A STRANGE INCIDENT HAPPENED DURING MAY 5, THE FIRST DAY OF THE BITTER BATTLE OF THE WILDERNESS.

KEY CONFEDERATE GENERALS LEE, HILL, AND STUART FOUND THEMSELVES CUT OFF IN A SMALL CLEARING.

FIGHTING IN THE WOODLAND WAS CONFUSING AND NEITHER SIDE KNEW WHERE THEIR OWN MEN WERE.

A GROUP OF UNION SOLDIERS EMERGED ON THE OTHER SIDE OF THE CLEARING. THEY WERE WITHIN FIRING DISTANCE OF THE CONFEDERATE GENERALS.

THE UNION OFFICER COULD HAVE ORDERED HIS MEN TO SHOOT THE CONFEDERATE GENERALS. INSTEAD, HE ORDERED HIS MEN TO RETREAT INTO THE WOODS.

MEN! ABOUT TURN!

WE WILL NEVER KNOW WHY HE SAVED THE THREE GREAT CONFEDERATE LEADERS.

AS THE GUNS FIRED, THE AIR FILLED WITH MUZZLE FLASH, SMOKE, AND SPARKS. THE SMOKE MADE IT IMPOSSIBLE TO SEE.

SPARKS FROM THE GUNS SET FIRE TO THE DRY, THICK VEGETATION OF THE WILDERNESS.

AS FIRES BROKE OUT, SOLDIERS ON BOTH SIDES RAN FROM THE FLAMES. MANY WOUNDED SOLDIERS HAD TO BE LEFT ON THE BATTLEFIELD.

AAARGH!

HELP! WE'RE ALL GOING TO DIE OUT HERE!

HUNDREDS OF SOLDIERS ON BOTH SIDES DIED IN THE FOREST FIRES, WHICH BURNED INTO THE NIGHT.

AMMUNITION THAT THE SOLDIERS HAD BEEN CARRYING EXPLODED, FILLING THE AIR WITH THE CRACK OF GUNFIRE.

KRAK! BOOM! SPANG!

THIS PLACE IS HELL! OUR MEN ARE BURNING TO DEATH IN THERE!

GENERAL LEE WILL HELP US. HE'LL KNOW WHAT TO DO.

AT 1:00 A.M. ON MAY 6, 1864, GENERAL LONGSTREET AND HIS MEN BEGAN TO MARCH TOWARD THE WILDERNESS. GENERAL LEE BELIEVED THAT THE CONFEDERATE ARMY COULD NOT DEFEAT THE UNION FORCES WITHOUT LONGSTREET AND HIS MEN.

LONGSTREET'S I CORPS MADE UP ONE-THIRD OF GENERAL LEE'S ARMY. HE HOPED THAT THEIR ARRIVAL, EARLY IN THE MORNING OF MAY 6, WOULD TURN THE TIDE OF THE BATTLE IN HIS FAVOR.

BOTH ARMIES HAD TRIED TO FORM DEFENSIVE LINES IN THE WILDERNESS. BUT THE DENSE WOODLAND PREVENTED THE SOLDIERS FROM KNOWING WHERE THEY WERE IN RELATION TO EACH OTHER.

DEFENSIVE LINES WERE SHORT AND BROKEN.

AT 5:00 A.M., THREE OF UNION GENERAL HANCOCK'S DIVISIONS, WITH SUPPORT FROM GENERALS GETTYS AND WADSWORTH, FORMED A DETERMINED LINE OF ATTACK ON THE ORANGE PLANK ROAD.

THIS FIERCE UNION ATTACK OVERWHELMED GENERAL HILL'S CONFUSED CONFEDERATE TROOPS AND THEY BEGAN TO RETREAT.

HILL'S MEN ARE IN TROUBLE. ORDER THE SUPPLY TRAIN TO MAKE READY FOR A RETREAT.

WHERE *IS* LONGSTREET WHEN I NEED HIM?

A MESSENGER WAS SENT TO LONGSTREET TO ORDER HIM TO RUSH HIS TROOPS TO THE BATTLEFIELD.

WE MUST RALLY THE MEN AND HOPE THEY CAN HOLD UNTIL LONGSTREET BRINGS HIS REINFORCEMENTS.

HANCOCK'S FLANKING MOVE CIRCLED THE CONFEDERATE LINE FROM THE NORTH AND SOUTH.

THIS LEFT THE CONFEDERATE FORCES WITH NOWHERE TO GO BUT BACKWARD OR FORWARD INTO THE FIRING LINE.

CONFEDERATE ARTILLERY TO THE NORTH OF THE ORANGE PLANK ROAD WERE SLOWING DOWN GENERAL HANCOCK'S MEN, BUT THEY COULD NOT STOP THEM COMPLETELY.

BOOM!

BOOM!

BE BRAVE, MEN!

UNION II CORPS BEGAN TO CREEP IN BEHIND THE CONFEDERATE ARTILLERY. THEY WERE IN A STRONG POSITION TO TRAP THE CONFEDERATES IN THE MIDDLE AND WIN THE BATTLE.

AT 6:30 A.M., GENERAL LONGSTREET'S CONFEDERATE REINFORCEMENTS FINALLY ARRIVED.

CONFEDERATE BRIGADIER GENERAL JOSEPH KERSHAW DROVE HIS MEN INTO THE WILDERNESS.

BE BRAVE, MEN!

KRAK! KRAK! KRAK!

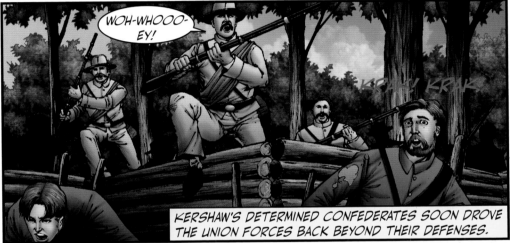

WOH-WHOOO-EY!

KRAK! KRAK

KERSHAW'S DETERMINED CONFEDERATES SOON DROVE THE UNION FORCES BACK BEYOND THEIR DEFENSES.

KRAK! KRAK

UNION SOLDIERS OF II CORPS WERE FORCED TO RETREAT UNDER THE FURY OF KERSHAW'S ATTACK.

THE TEXAS BRIGADE HAD FOUGHT MANY BATTLES AND LOST MANY MEN. ONLY 800 SOLDIERS SURVIVED FROM THE ORIGINAL BRIGADE, WHICH WAS ABOUT 3,500 MEN AT THE BEGINNING OF THE WAR.

GENERAL LEE WAS PARTICULARLY FOND OF THE TEXAS BRIGADE.

HURRAH FOR TEXAS!

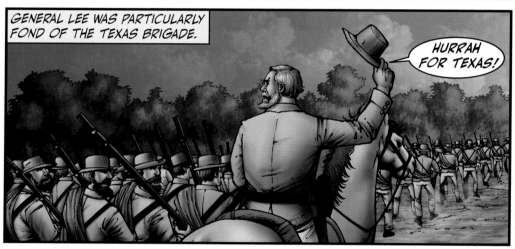

KRAK! KRAK! KRAK!

BOOM!

GENERAL LEE WANTED TO LEAD GENERAL GREGG'S TEXANS IN THE BATTLE. LEE KNEW THE MEN WERE IN DANGER, AND HE WANTED TO TAKE AN ACTIVE PART IN THE FIGHT.

LET'S *CHARGE*, TEXAS!

WE WON'T GO ON UNLESS YOU GO BACK!

I WOULD CHARGE HELL ITSELF FOR THAT OLD MAN.

BUT THE TEXANS WERE HORRIFIED THAT LEE WOULD PUT HIMSELF IN SUCH DANGER.

LEE TURNED HIS HORSE RELUCTANTLY AND WENT TO THE REAR OF THE BATTLEFIELD.

THE TEXANS CHARGED INTO BATTLE.

FORWARD, BRAVE TEXANS!

DESTROY THE YANKEES!

AT TAPP FIELD, THE TEXANS LOST MORE THAN HALF THEIR MEN IN JUST A FEW MINUTES. YET THEY MANAGED TO HOLD THE UNION FORCES AT BAY.

BOOM! KRAK!

KRAK! BOOM!

AAARRGH!

HANCOCK'S MEN RENEWED THEIR ATTACK WITH VIGOR, BUT LONGSTREET HAD 20,000 MEN TO ORDER INTO BATTLE.

THE CONFEDERATE FORCES HELD A *STRONG LINE* AND STOPPED THE ENEMY FROM ADVANCING.

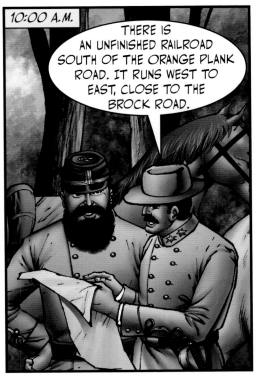

10:00 A.M.

THERE IS AN UNFINISHED RAILROAD SOUTH OF THE ORANGE PLANK ROAD. IT RUNS WEST TO EAST, CLOSE TO THE BROCK ROAD.

IF WE SEND MEN ALONG THE TRACK, WE CAN ATTACK THE LEFT FLANK OF THE UNION FORCES FROM THE SOUTH. IT'S PERFECT!

SORRELL, GATHER AS MANY MEN AS YOU CAN FIND AND TAKE THEM EAST ALONG THIS RAILROAD TRACK.

ENGAGE THE ENEMY WITH FULL FORCE.

SORRELL PUT TOGETHER AN ARMY MADE UP OF SCATTERED BRIGADES FROM GEORGIA, MISSISSIPPI, AND VIRGINIA.

HE HAD NEVER BEFORE COMMANDED TROOPS IN COMBAT.

SORRELL MARCHED HIS MEN ALONG THE RAILROAD. BY 11:30 A.M. THEY WERE IN POSITION TO ATTACK THE UNION LEFT FLANK.

SORRELL'S MEN CAUGHT THE UNION FORCES COMPLETELY OFF GUARD.

WOH-WHOOO-EY!

RALLY YOUR MEN FOR A FULL FRONTAL ATTACK ON THE UNION LINE.

YES, SIR!

CHARGE!

THE CONFEDERATE ATTACK WAS SO FIERCE THAT MANY UNION INFANTRYMEN BROKE RANKS AND RAN FOR COVER.

KRAK! KRAK! KRAK!

OTHERS HELD THEIR GROUND.

FIRE!

KRAK! KRAK!

IN PARTICULAR, THE 20TH MASSACHUSETTS MADE A BRAVE BUT DESPERATE ATTEMPT TO HOLD THEIR LINE.

THEY WERE DETERMINED NOT TO GIVE UP.

YET THEY WERE MASSACRED BY THE ONCOMING CONFEDERATES.

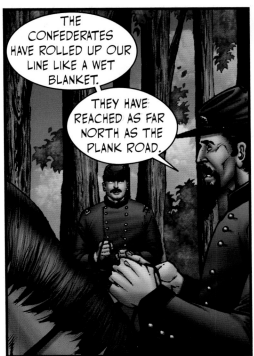

THE CONFEDERATES HAVE ROLLED UP OUR LINE LIKE A WET BLANKET.

THEY HAVE REACHED AS FAR NORTH AS THE PLANK ROAD.

WE WILL HAVE AS GREAT A SUCCESS AS "STONEWALL" JACKSON HIMSELF. THIS WILL BE *MY* BATTLE OF CHANCELLORSVILLE!

AS LONGSTREET AND HIS OFFICERS RODE THROUGH THE WILDERNESS, THEY CAME UNDER FIRE.

WHILE DIRECTING GENERAL JENKINS'S MEN INTO A RETURN ASSAULT, GENERAL LONGSTREET WAS CAUGHT IN FRIENDLY FIRE.

BRIGADIER GENERAL MICAH JENKINS WAS SHOT AND KILLED.

GENERAL LONGSTREET, BRIGADIER GENERAL JENKINS, AND THEIR STAFF WERE ACCIDENTALLY FIRED ON BY DISORIENTATED CONFEDERATE INFANTRYMEN.

IT WAS A TERRIBLE AND COSTLY MISTAKE.

LONGSTREET WAS COMMANDER OF I CORPS AND A VALUABLE OFFICER IN LEE'S ARMY. IT WOULD TAKE HIM SIX MONTHS TO RECOVER FROM HIS INJURIES.

WITHOUT GENERAL LONGSTREET THE CONFEDERATE ATTACK STOPPED IN ITS TRACKS. GENERAL LEE QUICKLY CALLED ON MAJOR GENERAL RICHARD ANDERSON.

ANDERSON, LONGSTREET IS HURT. BUT WE CANNOT STOP THIS ATTACK. I NEED YOU TO REGROUP AND RALLY THE MEN.

THE REBEL ATTACK IS FALTERING. REGROUP AND SEND FOR REINFORCEMENTS. WE WILL WIN THIS BATTLE *YET!*

IT WAS 4:00 P.M. BEFORE THE CONFEDERATES WERE READY TO RESUME THEIR ATTACK.

BUT THE ELEMENT OF SURPRISE GENERATED BY LONGSTREET'S ORIGINAL ASSAULT WAS NOW LOST.

GENERAL LEE SENT 13 BRIGADES TO ATTACK HANCOCK AND BURNSIDE'S SPLINTERED UNION TROOPS.

KRAK!-KRAK! KRAK! BANG!

THE UNION ARMY USED THE TIME BETWEEN ATTACKS TO BRING UP SUPPORTING ARTILLERY.

THEY ALSO BUILT CRUDE BREASTWORKS AND USED THEM AS A DEFENSE AGAINST THE CONFEDERATE ATTACK.

AS ON THE PREVIOUS DAY, MUZZLE FLASH AND HOT AMMUNITION BEGAN TO SET FIRE TO THE UNDERGROWTH ON THE BATTLEFIELD.

THE UNION BREASTWORKS HAD BEEN BUILT USING EARTH, LOGS, BRANCHES, AND BRUSH.

FIRES IMMEDIATELY RIPPED THROUGH THE BREASTWORKS.

FIRE! FIRE!

QUICKLY WITHDRAW, MEN!

THE UNION INFANTRY RETREATED, NOT IN DEFEAT, BUT TO SAVE THEMSELVES FROM THE BURNING BREASTWORKS.

THE CONFEDERATE FORCES ALSO HAD TO BACK AWAY FROM THE FIRES.

RUN!

AS BOTH SIDES RETREATED, THEY TOOK WITH THEM AS MANY WOUNDED AS THEY COULD CARRY.

HANCOCK WAS ORDERED TO COUNTERATTACK AT 6.00 P.M. BUT HIS MEN WERE VERY LOW ON AMMUNITION. THEIR FIGHTING WAS OVER.

AT SUNDOWN, CONFEDERATE GENERAL GORDON'S II CORPS WERE IN POSITION TO ATTACK THE UNION RIGHT FLANK.

GENERAL BURNSIDE'S UNION TROOPS ON THE RIGHT FLANK WERE TAKEN BY SURPRISE. THEY WERE NOT PREPARED FOR THE FIERCE FIGHTING THAT FOLLOWED.

DROP YOUR WEAPONS!

THEY CRUMBLED UNDER THE ATTACK.

GENERAL GORDON CAPTURED 600 MEN AND TWO UNION GENERALS.

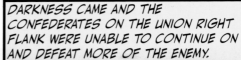

DARKNESS CAME AND THE CONFEDERATES ON THE UNION RIGHT FLANK WERE UNABLE TO CONTINUE ON AND DEFEAT MORE OF THE ENEMY.

GENTLEMEN...

THE BATTLE IS OVER, GENERAL GRANT. BOTH OUR LEFT AND RIGHT FLANKS ARE DESTROYED.

WE HAVE LOST THIS BATTLE, SIR.

YET WE ARE NOTHING DAUNTED, GENTLEMEN.

THE CONFEDERATES COULD COUNT THE BATTLE OF THE WILDERNESS A SUCCESS IN STRATEGIC TERMS...

...YET THE ARMY OF NORTHERN VIRGINIA HAD LOST 7,500 VALUABLE MEN IN THE PROCESS.

NOW WE MUST WAIT FOR THE UNION ARMY TO RETREAT BACK ACROSS THE RIVER, AND PREPARE OURSELVES FOR THE NEXT GREAT BATTLE.

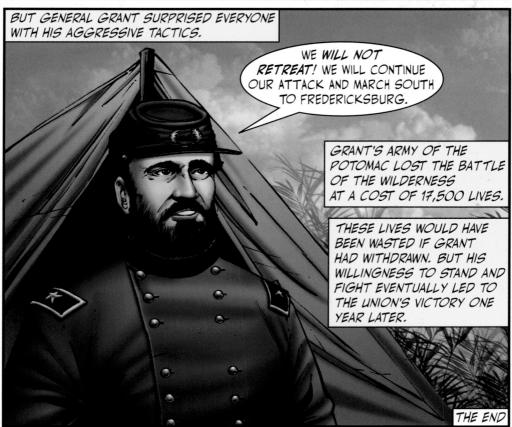

BUT GENERAL GRANT SURPRISED EVERYONE WITH HIS AGGRESSIVE TACTICS.

WE *WILL NOT RETREAT!* WE WILL CONTINUE OUR ATTACK AND MARCH SOUTH TO FREDERICKSBURG.

GRANT'S ARMY OF THE POTOMAC LOST THE BATTLE OF THE WILDERNESS AT A COST OF 17,500 LIVES.

THESE LIVES WOULD HAVE BEEN WASTED IF GRANT HAD WITHDRAWN. BUT HIS WILLINGNESS TO STAND AND FIGHT EVENTUALLY LED TO THE UNION'S VICTORY ONE YEAR LATER.

THE END

# AFTERMATH

On the night of May 7, Grant's army was on the move. It headed south, toward Spotsylvania Court House, on Lee's road to Richmond. If Grant arrived there first, Lee would have to attack.

When the tired Union troops realized Grant's plan, their morale was boosted. They weren't retreating; they were simply positioning themselves for another battle with Lee. They marched all night. However, Lee saw what the Union army was doing and marched his men all night, too. He got to Spotsylvania just ahead of Grant. The battle that followed raged for twelve days, ending with Grant pulling his troops out of the battlefield —yet still ready to continue his chase of Lee.

In the following weeks, the opposing armies were in constant contact with one another. After Spotsylvania, many smaller battles were fought. This series of battles, starting with the Wilderness, became known as the "Overland Campaign." In the first month of the campaign, Grant lost about 60,000 men, and yet Lee's army was not broken—and it was still on the move.

People in the North were growing weary of the terrible losses its army was suffering under Grant. To many, it seemed as if the war would never end. Yet Grant's strategy was paying off. By keeping Lee on the move, it made it impossible for the Confederate general to launch strong attacks

Soldier Robert Stoddard Robertson later described the Wilderness as "the strangest and most undescribable battle in history. A battle which no man saw, and in which artillery was useless and hardly used at all." The bitter fighting stopped Grant from advancing, but unfortunately for Lee, he did not retreat. (Courtesy of Library of Congress)

▼

▲

Generals Lee and Grant met again at the battle of Spotsylvania House, a brutal battle which went on for 12 days and was one of the most violent battles of the entire war, with many losses. (Courtesy of Library of Congress)

General Longstreet was one of Lee's most valued generals. Longstreet was out of action for over six months following the severe injuries he suffered at the Wilderness. This was a huge blow to Lee's battle plans. (Courtesy of Lee Fendall-House)

▼

of his own. Although Lee's army was not broken and Richmond was not captured, the grinding down of the Confederate war effort was becoming a success.

A series of Union victories beginning in late 1864 were the first true signs of the war's end. Victories at Mobile Bay, Alabama; General Sherman's capture of Atlanta; and the Union siege of Petersburg, Virginia, contributed to the beginning of the end for the South.

By the spring of 1865, the South could no longer continue to fight. It was worn out by an opponent who although had suffered far greater losses, had far greater numbers of men to fight. In April 1865, Lee surrendered to Grant at Appomattox Court House, Virginia, ending long four years of conflict.

# GLOSSARY

**artillery**   Large, heavy guns that are mounted on wheels or tracks.

**breastworks**   Temporary fortifications.

**brigade**   A large army unit.

**continuously**   Keeping on without stopping.

**daunt**   To cause to lose courage.

**desert**   To go away from someone or something one has a duty to stay with our support.

**disorient**   To cause to lose the sense of time, place, or identity.

**earthworks**   A mound or other construction made of earth; often used as a fortification on a battlefield.

**engage**   To take part or involve oneself.

**junction**   The place where things join or meet.

**muzzle**   The front of a gun barrel.

**rally**   To gather or join together in support of a common cause.

**rear guard**   A military detachment detailed to bring up and protect the rear of a main body or force.

**reluctantly**   Doing something unwillingly.

**scrub growth**   Small trees or shrubs

**skirmish**   A minor fight between small bodies of troops.

**splinter**   To break apart.

**thicket**   A heavy growth of plants, bushes, or small trees.

▲

Lieutenant General Grant (left) was possibly the best all-round soldier of the American Civil War, and far surpassed the achievements of his leader, General George Meade (right). The purple battle flag behind them was used for the first time at the battle of the Wilderness. (Ron Volstad © Osprey Publishing Ltd)

# FOR MORE INFORMATION

## ORGANIZATIONS

**The National Civil War Museum**
One Lincoln Circle at Reservoir Park
P.O. Box 1861
Harrisburg, PA 17105-1861
001 (717) 260 1861
Website:
http://www.nationalcivilwarmuseum.org/

**The National Park Service**
**Fredericksburg and Spotsylvania**
**National Military Park**
Fredericksburg, VA
001 (540) 373 6122
Website:
http://www.nps.gov/frsp/wild.htm

## FOR FURTHER READING

Coffin, Howard. *The Battered Stars: One State's Civil War Ordeal During Grant's Overland Campaign.* Woodstock, VT: Countryman Press, 2002.

Dean-Sheehan, Aaron and James McPherson. *Struggle For a Vast Future.* Oxford, England: Osprey Publishing, 2006.

Gallagher, Gary W. (editor). *The Wilderness Campaign.* Chapel Hill, NC: University of North Carolina Press, 1997.

McWhiney, Grady. *Battle in the Wilderness: Grant Meets Lee.* Abilene, TX: McWhiney Foundation Press, 1995.

The battle of the Wilderness, "one of the most desperate battles of modern times," led to a completely new type of warfare. Faced with dense woodland, and no set lines of defense, both sides had to think of new ways to defeat the enemy. (Courtesy of Library of Congress)

▼

# INDEX